Dhawana
The Story of a Nature-spirit
By Atem

Copyright © 2023

The moral right to be identified as the creators of the work has been asserted by them in accordance with the Copyright, Designs and Patents Act 1988. All rights reserved.

No part of this book may be reproduced, stored in a retrieval system or transmitted in any form or by any means, electronic, mechanical, photocopying, recording or otherwise, without the prior permission of the authors.

Designed by Red Feather Publishing

www.redfeather.com.au

ISBN: 978-0-6459581-1-9

Contents

Preface	3
1. How it All Began	6
2. Dhawana	16
3. Another Farewell	23
4. The Rabbits	29
5. The Miracle	38
6. Excerpts from a Diary	48
7. Intermezzo	55
8. The Message	63
9. Where is Dhawana?	70
10. Dhawana's Narration	76
11. Dhawana Continues	80
12. Back Again in Europe	89

13.	Dhawana's New Life	97
14.	The Surprise Visit	108
15.	The Rebirth	113
Also By Atem		122

As the real names of friends and relatives in this book have been transposed into fictitious ones, I thought it only proper to convert my own name as well. Therefore, you'll meet 'Roma' along the way. I'm sure you won't mind!

To Kristie and Rob

Preface

The impalpable, the invisible, the inaudible. For how long now have these been a target of disbelief, cynicism and scepticism? Unfamiliar to most of us, but nevertheless part of the awe-inspiring, never ceasing creation, we give it little thought, if any at all. Could it be that the impalpable, the invisible, the inaudible represent the real world, a world where the real criteria predominate, in contradistinction to our own eclipsed annihilating complexity?

There is no denying that over the years, our senses have rapidly increased. Our own substantiality is a conglomerate of vibrations, and we take it for granted without any scruples. Do we still have to rack our brains over whether different levels of vibrations do exist, vibrations encompassing us, protecting or even pervading us? Science is taking such gigantic steps that we cannot digest any more. But in the end, it will be science that conquers the question marks that are still mysteries today. Let's hope that the breakthroughs won't be too distant.

In the following pages, we'll encounter the story of a nature-spirit: Dhawana. For him and his co-workers, life in this world does not overwhelm them as it does us, simply because they are much further evolved in understanding nature's workings.

Doubtless, we human beings ought to be more aware of possessing our own special sense for seeing and conversing with nature-spirits. It lies inherent in all of us, and this faculty is by no means mysterious. The secret simply lies in the fact that we do not try! Nature-spirits are very concerned about us and about what we, as inconsiderate humans, are doing. They are much closer to people than we can ever imagine.

How then shall we look upon Dhawana's life story? May I suggest with joy, with our long-lost childhood happiness, with surrender to the beauty of a world that most of us do not know about? For a while, we'll forget about that which for ages has occupied our beings, our thoughts, generally presenting us with a mixture of sadness, joy, pain, happiness, unhappiness and so on.

Before I conclude this introduction, I wish to draw your attention to the well-established fact of the UFO phenomenon. Does belief only come when we see with our own eyes? Are thousands, no millions of people imagining things? The files of evidence are now so enormous that, whether we want it or not, we cannot deny it any longer.

And so, one day, it will be the same with the unseen worlds around us. Until then, you may happily look upon Dhawana's story as a fairy-tale. But if at all possible, I would rather like you to see it as a newly opened road of beauty, warmth, deep feeling, and care for us all. Because it really did happen exactly as I described it, and I am proud and extremely thankful for the wealth of happiness it has given me, and others w ith me.

1

HOW IT ALL BEGAN

What do you expect when you go out looking for a nature-spirit in the Australian bush? Nothing, of course. Or maybe, subconsciously, you search for a little elf, or some gnomes. But *this*, no, this was the last thing we expected.

First, however, I would like to ask you to go with me through the introductory section, as it forms part and parcel of the entire matter. It all began far from Australia. There, in a small European country, we lived in a big old house, together with three wonderful young people: Ross and Katie who were married, and Enco, a friend. We shall certainly meet them later in the book.

The house in Europe

There was also a large wood belonging to the house, and this is what I mainly intend talking about at this moment. Leaving the house, we first had to follow a path through the shrubs, then pass a very old, old beech tree beside a long since abandoned tennis court. Following that, we came to a tiny paddock, with grass growing abundantly and unrestrictedly. During the summer, it was dotted with flowers such as buttercups, daisies and other flowers. Having arrived there, we could see the wood stretching in front of us in all its impressive glory. But we were still separated from it, the dividing line being a little stream, across which a dear but somewhat mouldered little bridge was to be f ound.

The rustic bridge, leading into the wood

Late one warm summer evening, we sat ourselves down in the grass, just a little left of the bridge along the footpath, admiring the stillness and the atmosphere of the woods. Then suddenly, at the opposite side of the path between some low-growing bushes along the water edge, I saw four little beings looking at us in an inquisitive but friendly way. Gnomes by the look of them: a man, a woman and two smaller ones, probably younger in age. How odd, I thought, I have never seen any such thing in all my life. I told Bor, my husband sitting next to me about it, but although he tried hard to see them, to his great disappointment, he did not succeed.

Well, I thought after some time, why not ask them what they are doing there, staring at us. Nothing can be lost if they won't answer. So, we said: "Is there any reason why you lovely people are standing here? Is there something you wish to convey to us?"

A broad smile appeared on the gnome-man's face and he nodded emphatically.

"What is it then?" I asked, now more intrigued by the whole affair.

He pointed at the bridge, and so did the other three, but nothing was said. So, there was only one way left open to us, we had to continue asking questions.

"The bridge," I said. "Do you want to tell us it would be dangerous to cross the bridge from now on?"

Intensive denials came from all four of them. So this didn't seem to be the case at all. Then Bor stepped in.

"I have a feeling," he said, "that they sort of belong to the bridge."

Suddenly their faces indicated approval.

"Ah," we said. "Now we are on the right path. Let's see what comes out of that."

Now their faces lit up with joyful expectation.

"You belong to the little bridge, don't you? Could it be that you are its guardians?"

Again, they nodded in accordance, but their faces still held that expression of expectation. What now?

Again, Bor happened to find an answer. "Probably we have to ask for their approval before entering the wood by crossing the bridge," he said, and the gnome family responded happily to this. Soon after that they all disappeared, together with the evening light, so that we were almost left in the dark.

The next morning, we couldn't help returning the same spot, and although we could not discover our little friends again at the side of the bridge, we obediently asked permission to enter the wood by way of the bridge. It seemed as if a strong feeling of approval came to us from over the water, and thus we crossed the bridge, completely at ease in our minds.

At this point, I should say that this wood, twenty hectares of it, had never been open to the public. And naturally, in an unspoiled wood like this, the fairy life must have been particularly rich. Walking over the main path, strewn with leaves, fallen year after year after year from the many beech trees bordering it, we talked about the previous night's experience, wondering about the workings of nature's life in g eneral.

"Would there be someone here in charge of it all?" Bor asked. "A chief, a leader, or whatever you might call it?"

"Yes, who knows," I said. "Shall we investigate and see if we can find something?"

What else could we do than spy around, looking here, looking there, but with no result. At last, we sat ourselves down on the top of a small hill, disappointed, but understanding that one cannot force a thing like that, not even with the best of intentions. Then, suddenly, we both felt as if there was something behind us. We turned around, and yes, there he was, hesitantly, at quite some distance: a slender figure, quite different from the ones we had seen the night before. Dressed in what looked like a tight black costume, a funny little round black hat, with its brim turned slightly upward on his head. He was bigger in stature, though, from the gnomes we'd seen before, and certainly more elegant, with a delicately shaped face.

"It's an elf," I told Bor, and this time too, he had to believe me, because he himself could clearly feel its presence.

The shy figure did not show any intention of coming closer to us, therefore the best thing to do, I thought, was to send him our hearty greetings, combined with assurances of our best intentions, and ask him to favour us by telling us his name. The answer came after a few moments of consideration: "My name is PARMA," he said, and after that he quickly disappeared like a gentle breeze.

How enthusiastically we walked home, more than content with the results of the day. We would never forget him, even if we never saw him again. It was as if the wood was looking brighter, the birds singing more melodiously, the air more peaceful than before.

Shortly after, the time came for us to leave this little country for our new life in Australia. Our second immigration as a matter of fact, and therefore, we were not all unfamiliar with the country we were going to call our homeland again. On the last day before our departure, we decided to go to the wood again and say farewell to Parma. This time, before crossing the bridge, we saw two of the little gnomes again, the man and the woman, standing guard at the side. They were fervently nodding their heads as if to affirm our yet unspoken question for approval to enter their kingdom. When we arrived at the hill where we had previously seen him, we saw Parma, a little closer to us than before. He sort of gestured to us to walk on, which we could not quite understand. Our time was very limited as we still had to pack and say farewell to some friends. But on the other hand, we thought it also impolite not to respond to Parma's wish, so we were about to continue our walk, when suddenly, he sent us the following message: "Please make sure to return along this self-same path."

Ah! That was at least something! Thus, we walked on for some time, further into the wood, and after arriving at the end, we turned and walked back along the same path, something we would not have done without Parma's request, as the path made a full circle through the wood, finishing up at the bridge. Having arrived at the hill again, there was nothing to be seen. But a little further, somewhat nearer to the bridge in a more open space between the trees, and a good fifty meters distance from the path, we saw them; Parma with all of his little friends, drawn up in a straight line to his left and to his right. When we became apparently visible to them, the whole company started to bow to us, very solemnly. We could not completely hide a smile, for it was such an unusual sight. But we bowed to them in return. (Just as well nobody could see us!) saying "Goodbye, goodbye, dear people. May God bless you and grant that we may see each other again."

After which, we thought the ceremony had come to an end. But no, they kept on standing there and bowing over and over again. Now we were at a loss. Surely, we could not go on like this, for then it would become quite ridiculous. Until Parma came to the rescue, saying, "Please, be so kind to walk on. If you keep on standing there, we will have to turn our backs to you in order to go our different ways. And that's something we do not want to do, as we find this very impolite. Thank you for giving us your friendship, and kindly pass on our greetings to the nature-spirits in your new country, if possible."

Completely astonished, not only by so much courtesy — how much we still had to learn! — but also by this unexpected speech, we once more greeted them all, then continued our walk home, afraid of causing some more bowing activities. And so, we ended our first episode. We little expected how dramatically our next meeting would turn out.

2

Dhawana

I won't bother you with all the details concerning our trip by plane to Australia; how we stayed, after arriving there for two weeks at my son Maurice's place; how we rented a house, awaiting the arrival of our furniture sent over by container ship; how we found, just in the nick of time, a lovely house just opposite National Park which we bought at once and where we soon established ourselves.

National Park: what a treasure we found it to be. But how big, how enormously big. Here, there was no thought of going for a walk and trying to find nature-spirits. The vastness of it all, the wild growth and also the not to be underestimated possibilities of meeting snakes, spiders, scorpions, and what not. No, we could not use the same tactics, although unwittingly applied as in our dear old woods before. The only way of going through National Park was by car, which we undertook one warm Sunday morning after about two months of hard work, getting everything in order for the beginning of our new life. No use looking for a repeat of our former adventures. So, we gave up. Better to forget it altogether, we thought.

We had taken lunch and coffee with us, and at a certain spot along the road, Bor stopped the car, and we took our sandwiches and poured the coffee, still sitting in the car. It was a lovely, calm day, and not a soul to be seen. Talking about everyday happenings, our thoughts far away from things unseen, we suddenly heard something tap on the boot of the car. A falling branch, we thought, neither of us bothering to say it aloud. A little later, the same sound, but now against the back window. We both looked surprised. In fact, as we were not parked under any tree whatsoever, it could not have been a branch after all. And furthermore, there was no wind. But we left it at that and continued with our lunch and conversation.

Again, this noise at the back, not once, but continuously, as if someone was tapping against our car with a stone.

The spot where the knocking on the car took place

"What's going on?" we said at last, and Bor got out to investigate. Nothing... Also, nothing to be seen in the bush around us, which happened to be quite open and easily observed. He got back into the car again, but this tapping became so consistent that we could no longer ignore it.

"This is too uncanny for words," Bor remarked. "Let's both get out of the car and see what's going on."

From the point where we were standing, a small path led into the bush, so we decided to lock the car and follow the path. After some one hundred metres, we found a lovely spot, where a somewhat blackened tree stump stood, completely grown into a corkscrew in the midst of an open space. The whole place was in what one might describe as a little valley, or a rather secluded hollow, as it was not so very big. We stood still, admiring the unusual growth of the tree. We did not dare go much further, as the Australian bush is known for its impenetrability, and furthermore, we did not want to get ourselves lost.

But then it happened; good Lord! What a giant he was! As I said in the very beginning, this was the last thing we would ever have expected. With enormous steps, he came out of the bush. It was as if you could hear the branches cracking, the leaves rustling, although he did not seem to touch anything at all. Petrified, I tried to describe it as much as I could to Bor, who also stood, as if rooted to the ground. No, it was not an elf, not by far, neither was it a gnome or fairy. This was more, much more. It resembled a human being, yes, certainly almost a copy of an Australian Aboriginal. But so big, goodness me, I estimated him to be over seven feet tall. And his feet, unbelievable: coal-shovels we would call them, but as flat as a pair of flippers. His hair was bushy, seemingly held together by a hairband. And then his face: big but friendly, eyes that laughed, teeth so big and white that you wouldn't believe it. He kept on laughing at us, thus trying to put us at ease, until at last we unbent a little, surrendering to his friendliness and forgetting about the shock he had given us.

"I am DHAWANA," he said at last, with profound emphasis on the letter H after the D of his name. We hastened to convey greetings to him from his nature companion Parma in the far-away country, but he seemed to know all about it. Heaven knows how.

He turned out to be a nature-spirit, for soon he invited us to step down into the hollow, where on the other side we saw, peeping through the undergrowth, the laughing faces of some other creatures, much smaller though, I would say about two feet high, no more. Their outward appearance differed completely from that of Dhawana's, their colouring being much lighter — Dhawana being almost black – and they seemed to delight in draping themselves with the most garishly coloured clothes.

"They are a constant worry to me," Dhawana said to us. "They are supposed to work all day, looking after everything that needs to be done in this great, big park. But all they do is play, play, play. It gives me a pain. I can't cope with them anymore."

Now we laughed, completely relaxed. And when he also laughed, he showed us the house where the little beings lived. In actual fact, you couldn't really call it a house. It was a long and stretched out thing, consisting of only a narrow roof, resting on a lot of rough-looking little poles.

"That's what they've spent their efforts on," Dhawana sighed, but we felt that in his heart, he didn't mind it so much.

It was as if we had known him for ages. His hugeness we didn't mind any more. He was our friend, a fact that we could be certain of. And that we had not seen the last of him, was also sure. What strange things were going to happen, but of that we were still completely ignorant.

The hollow with the cork-screwed tree, Dhawana's headquarters in National Park

3

Another Farewell

Next time we went to what we soon called 'Dhawana's Headquarters', we could not discover him anywhere. Therefore, as we had taken our lunches again, we now put our folding chairs just along the edge of the hollow place in the bush. We enjoyed sitting in the warm sunshine for about half an hour and were just preparing to leave, when suddenly, I saw Dhawana at quite a distance walking through the undergrowth. He did not notice us, or at least he tried to give that impression, although I am quite sure he had shown himself deliberately. We understood. 'Do not think that I'll come as soon as you command me to,' was what he seemed to convey. And all the more we felt his strong-willed personality. I think it was just a matter of balancing attitudes against each other that day.

'It is all alright,' we sent out to him, away in the distance. Whereupon he suddenly raised his arm in a friendly gesture and disappeared into the bushes, out of our field of vision.

Several times after, we visited the place again, but to no avail. Neither Dhawana, nor one of his helpers were to be found. We thought it quite logical. The park is so immense, and they have their work spread out over such a large area that we should not be of so much importance to them. How wrong this actually turned out to be.

After five months in Australia, we had planned to go back to Europe for three months. Another busy time ahead. Our plane was leaving on the Monday, therefore we planned to go once more to Dhawana's place in order to say goodbye to him, if possible, on the Sunday morning previous to the day of departure. The rest of the day was to be taken up with other commitments, and thus this was the only chance left. On the point of entering our car, four visitors came down the driveway, happy, cheerful, wanting to say farewell. What else could we do? Absolutely nothing. So, we made the best of it, and when they had left, we looked at each other, knowing that our last chance of seeing Dhawana was utterly lost. So, we sat on the terrace, looking out into the forest at the other side of the road, not knowing what to do.

The terrace where Dhawana visited us on the Sunday morning

Dhawana's place was situated at quite a fair distance, and we certainly could not make it anymore. Then Bor said, "Do you think Dhawana would come here, to our place, if we could get a message across to him? Shall we try?"

"Why not? We have nothing to lose if we fail."

Silently we settled ourselves in easy chairs on the terrace and together we asked Dhawana to come to our place, as we could not make it to his.

Now, the road separating our house from the forest is a rather busy one, with cars passing all day. What were we doing asking Dhawana to cross this road? It was ridiculous and selfish; how could we do such a thing? And, of course, nothing good could come out of this. Serves us right, we said to each other. We decided to linger on for a while and then start attending to the things which still had to be done. For a moment, it was very quiet on the road, not a car to be seen. And then he came, crossing the road carefully, not at all happy, his mood nearly tangible. He stood between the plants bordering our terrace.

It is funny, but nature-spirits invariably seem to keep to places with plants and trees, rather than to paved terraces like ours, or too close to human beings. I think I'm not far wrong in presuming our vibrations not to be the same quality as theirs, and that we could do them some harm by coming to close to them. That is, I am sure, the main reason why they always keep their distance. This time, however, Dhawana stood closer to us than we had ever seen him. A trifle ironically, I thought, he made a deep bow, deeper than one generally bows to someone else, and slowly, emphatically he said, "My Lord... My Lady... Kindly convey my heartfelt greetings to Lord Parma."

Hastily we assured him of our readiness to fulfil his wish, at the same time apologizing for the inconveniences we had caused him by asking him to visit us. He accepted this gracefully, and his broad smile returned to his face, as if wanting to say, 'Its' not as bad as it looks, my friends.' Then another bow, this time executed in a more natural way, and off he went, moving quickly, majestically, despite his huge figure.

Enormously relieved, we now had something at least to take with us. It would have been so disappointing to visit Parma empty-handed. The rest of the day was filled with all sorts of activities, and the next day we boarded our plane, facing three months of a completely different way of life again in our little country in Europe.

4

THE RABBITS

"Bor, Bor!" cried Katie, running up the stairs to our room where we were staying on our return from Australia. "Oh Bor, Roma...", and almost out of breath she tumbled into the room and threw herself down in a chair.

"What is it, what is it?" we asked, startled by the sight of her pallid face.

She tried to compose herself a little. "That horrible man," she said and then she could not hold her tears anymore. Something seemed to ring a bell in me.

"That man in the big car we've just seen leaving?" I asked.

For, just before, I happened to stand at the window, and saw a big sordid looking man getting into a plush car, somewhat angrily talking to what I thought to be Enco.

"Yes... yes," Katie stuttered. "He's going to shoot all the rabbits in our forest."

"Oh come on, Katie, he cannot do that," Bor said. "It's private property, and nobody can do such a thing, you know that."

Just then Enco entered the room. "Huh," he snorted, "now we are in for something."

Then, bit by bit, the story came out. At that particular time, we were experiencing an unusually fierce winter, with constant snow and ice, and the animals in the woods had the greatest difficulty in finding food for themselves. Although things were put out for the birds every day, we nevertheless noticed that even birds had been eating birds, something which worried all of us. At the far end of the wood, separated by a wide moat, there was a nursery, dealing mostly in small shrubs. It now appeared that with the moat solidly frozen over, the rabbits of our forest were crossing the ice and happily eating the nursery's carefully planted shrubs. We all understood that this was a situation no one could have foreseen, and also that it meant a great loss to the nurseryman. Therefore, his complaints were well-founded, and we could appreciate this. On the other hand, his sudden threats and off-hand organising of a full-size shooting expedition, complete with huntsmen, hunting-dogs and all the rest of it, overwhelmed us completely.

Enco said: "First of all, let's stay calm. We'll spoil everything by losing our nerves."

"That's right," Bor said. "Good heavens, there must be plenty of ways to stop it."

"Yes," Katie agreed. "Let's set to work and try to defer it at least for a few days so that we can devise a plan."

Bor looked at me, and even without saying a single word, I knew exactly what he had in mind.

"Yes," I said. "Let's do that."

This was rather incomprehensible to the others present, but we soon explained.

"It may perhaps seem to be a rather poor contribution on our side," Bor said, "but Roma and I will go immediately to the forest and we'll try to find Parma. Those rabbits have to disappear for a while."

Katie and Enco were not in the least surprised. "Tell them," said Katie, "to go to the Centre, and I shall phone them to be prepared for the rabbits and to put out some food."

Now, talking in that way so seriously would normally cause raised eyebrows with the majority of people, but by now, all of us were so used to it that we didn't give it another thought. It should also be explained that what was called 'The Centre' actually represented our headquarters, a much bigger building than the one we occupied. Although it had its own forest, it was all governed by the same committee. Katie got up, fighting ready for action, running down the stairs to undertake some serious phoning, whilst Bor and I put on some extra warm clothing for our expedition to the forest. This was not an easy task. Everything was covered in snow and, even worse, with ice, which made walking an almost impossible business.

Snow in the woods

Carefully, oh so carefully, we made our way to the forest, though we already knew we would not be able to cross the little bridge. The bridge was, in fact, a heavily arched contraption and now so covered with ice that we would certainly have a nasty fall whilst trying to cross it. Nevertheless, we said we would worry about that when we arrived there, so we ploughed on until we reached our trouble-spot. Not quite, however. For, just before we came to the bridge, we happened to glance over the frozen water into the forest, pondering over how in heaven's name we would contrive to reach the woods, when suddenly I saw Parma on the other side of the stream. He was walking up and down, taking long strides and keeping his hands firmly clenched around the brim of his little black hat. Whether he saw us coming or not, we still do not know, engrossed as he was in his own thoughts, but I am sure he was waiting for us, although he did not show it.

"Parma!" we called at last. "Parma, we are here. We've come to help you. Please listen to us."

He stopped. Almost exhausted, he leaned against the trunk of a tree. No, we shall never forget the haunted look on his face — which I described to Bor — a look which convinced us forever how much harm we human beings could impose on nature-spirits by our hare-brained and egocentric behaviour.

Seeing him so agitated, we talked to him softly. "No one will be served by this," we said. "And certainly not the rabbits. Please Parma, please relax. We have devised a plan, you see."

With unbelieving eyes, he looked at us. Slowly, he let one hand drop from his hat, then also the other. What an unhappy picture he represented, and all the more we blessed the thought which had sent us on this mission.

"All is not lost, dear Parma," we said. "Listen… Do you think you could possibly tell the rabbits to flee to the forest belonging to 'the Centre'? It is not far, you know. Tell them to stay there till the danger-period is over. They will be received with love and fed. Meanwhile, we shall, all of us, do all we can on our side, buying plenty of food, but don't let them stay here during this day and tomorrow. As you have shown us in no uncertain manner, you seem to know all about what's going on. We do not have to beat around the bush. What do you say?"

Parma had visibly relaxed from his tense attitude. For a moment, a smile lit up his face. But soon his anxious expression returned.

"Fine," he said. "A marvellous idea. But what about the rabbits?"

"What about the rabbits?" we exclaimed in surprise. "We just told you: they have to go away for a little while. Disappear. Flee. Remove themselves!"

"I'm sorry," he answered. "What I mean is, rabbits, you know, they are rather stupid. Eating, eating, that's all they can think of, especially now, with this unusually severe winter. I don't know, I have strong doubts about them wanting to leave their burrows."

"Parma, how could you say such a thing? They'll come with dogs and ferrets; don't you see how serious this is? You, and all your helpers with you, you must be able to overcome this if you set your mind to it! First, take your time to regain your strength, become your own strong self again — for they won't come to disturb you before tomorrow — and you shall see it working out splendidly in no time."

More and more we saw Parma incline himself to our view. Then he bowed his head, kindly raised his hand, saluting us, and before we knew it, he had disappeared into the shrubs. Then, at last, we had an opportunity to look at each other.

"Oh dear God," I said, "what have we done? This will never work. Fancy, telling hundreds of rabbits to remove themselves for a few days to another place because they are in danger. It's too ridiculous, too incomprehensible..." and I nearly burst out laughing.

"Roma," Bor said disapprovingly. "If you start talking like that, it will have a negative effect on the entire enterprise. I know it's hard to believe in a thing like this, but we have to support them first of all in our minds. It's the only way out, believe me."

Very much ashamed, I agreed with him, but deep inside I had the greatest difficulty in convincing myself. We sludged back through the snow, all the way talking about our meeting with Parma on the other side of the stream in the wood.

5

THE MIRACLE

Katie, meanwhile, had contacted all sorts of people, as many as she could possibly think of, who could be of some help. In no time, several people were gathered in the sitting room: a police officer and his wife — good friends of Ross and Katie — a forest ranger well-rounded in forestry, and Mr. Richmond, also a friend. They all agreed that the first thing to be accomplished should be to achieve a postponement. And although it involved a great deal of persuasion, at last the nurseryman consented to leave things until Saturday — this being a Thursday. By that time, Ross had arrived home, and the next step to be undertaken was to contact a wholesale dealer in vegetables. Katie set herself diligently to this task, and after some time, she found someone willing to sell us ten cases of carrots for a reasonable price. It was a beginning, although the nurseryman did not accept this as a reason to stop his threatening attack. Bor promised to go and collect the carrots, and as at that moment a friend of ours just happened to call. The two of them set off together over the slippery, dangerous, icy roads to fulfil this part of the venture.

A wonderful, unexpected event must now be mentioned here, something which warmed our hearts as soon as we heard about it. When Bor and his friend told the greengrocer about the plight of the rabbits, this man spontaneously made them a gift of two hundred kilograms of apples, and thus, loaded with goods, they arrived home. Although darkness had already begun to set in, in no time, they put carrots and apples out at several places in the forest for the rabbits to eat instead of the nurseryman's precious shrubs. All we could do now was wait and hope for the best.

Ross and Mr. Richmond, carrying food for the rabbits

Ross and Mr. Richmond on the bridge, with carrots, apples, and straw for the rabbits

On the following day Siegfried, the police officer, arrived, bringing with him voluminous law-books and lots of impressive looking papers. This wonderful man appeared to have been working all through the night, studying every possible means concerning the rabbit problem, and the result of this was clearly visible in the pile of papers laying in front of him on the table. It did not take long to explain the look of concern on his face.

"Yes," he said, "according to the law, no one has a right to enter private property, and certainly not to start shooting, or whatever, without consent. But..." and here he hesitated for a while. "But in a case like this, where substantial damage and loss of income is obviously inflicted, the man is entitled to put a stop to it. And although we could go against him in all sorts of ways, in the end we shall have to give in, I'm afraid."

This certainly was a blow to the whole affair. However, in spite of it all, this self-same day turned out to be a day of all sorts of activities. The house was like a beehive, with people going in and out. Suggestions were being introduced left, right and centre, considered and then discarded as impracticable. At last, there was nothing else to do except to wait; wait and see what fate had in store for all of us and, above all, for the rabbits. A close inspection of the wood resulted in the discovery of the carrots and apples not having been touched at all, not a single one.

"They didn't find them," we decided despondently.

Katie on the slippery bridge during the heavy winter episode

Soon, all too soon, Saturday morning arrived. Tense with apprehension the house was awake early.

"Whatever happens," Ross said. "When they arrive, I shall go with them and keep an eye on things. No one can forbid this, I tell you." We all thought it very brave of Ross and highly admired him for it.

The shooting party arrived before you could say Jack Robinson. One car after another entered the grounds, stopping in front of the house and out came the heroic looking hunters, followed by their eager dogs. Ferrets were brought along, still held in their cages. Rifles were inspected, then shouldered, and at last they all set out for their special day's work. Ross had immediately joined them as we could see from our place at the windows, and soon we saw them disappear from our sight, knowing them to be set on achieving their goal and immensely enjoying it as a 'sport'. Deep in our hearts we could somehow understand it, but deeper still lived in us the feeling of having lost the battle altogether. Except for Bor and Katie, who kept on believing against all odds. Believing in what, we asked ourselves silently. Time was creeping on slowly, slower than a snail on holidays. Every now and then, we stole a glance through the windows, but all there was to be seen were the empty cars, a maddening sight, challenging us, I thought. Downstairs we heard Katie and Enco busying themselves with household activities, making coffee for all of us, trying to take their minds off what was happening, but not succeeding as was to be foreseen. Like proverbial cats on hot bricks, we all tried to fill in time. The clock seemed to derive satanical pleasure in moving its hands considerably slower than usual. Hour after hour passed by, and still no movement was to be perceived. Lunchtime was at hand and as we asked ourselves what in heaven's name kept them so long, we suddenly saw the whole procession emerge from the shrubs bordering the lane, quickly enter their vehicles and drive off. We stormed out of our room, tearing down the top stairs, just in time to meet Ross coming up the first flight of stairs. All of us hanging over the banisters, pelting him with ever so many questions. But Ross, unperturbed as always, quietly made his way up and met us all in th e passage of the first floor. We could not help, however, seeing a slight gleam of satisfaction crossing his face.

"Oh," he said somewhat carelessly. "Oh, believe it or not, but there was not a rabbit to be found in the entire forest."

It was like a bomb exploding. "What..?" we all yelled at the top of our voices. "What? Goodness gracious, Ross, tell us about it...!"

Ross uttered one of his inimitable chuckles, a sign of enjoying himself to the full.

"Well," he said, "at least I got them to agree not to start shooting at once, and to set out the dogs first to find the burrows. I thought this would take them considerable time to do. So they did, lots and lots of burrows they found. Of course, I couldn't stop them from sending the ferrets through the holes, and I thought that would be the end of it. They had also taken some nets with them, and they promised to catch the rabbits as soon as they appeared at the other end of their burrows, and not kill them. That was at least some comfort. But imagine! There was not a rabbit to be found. I couldn't believe it. Every burrow was empty, the ferrets rushing their way through the holes to no avail. What a farce it was! Hours and hours of work. I've never seen anything like it." And again, this chuckle of Ross's to close it all off.

In mute amazement, we stared at him, all of us. So that was why we saw the hunters entering their cars in such a subdued manner.

"Gee," said Katie, fighting a desire to burst out in tears, as I did, but soon laughing whole-heartedly with all the rest of us. We could not stop talking about it all day. Everyone who had assisted in this venture with so much warmth and feeling were told at once. Some hours later, the front-door bell rang. Enco went down to investigate and when he came up, with the broadest of grins on his face, he held in his hands a beautiful bouquet, delivered by the florist from the flower-shop.

'WITH THANKS FROM THE RABBITS', it said on the card attached to it.

"Mr. Richmond." Katie, Ross and Enco knew it at once, although no name was mentioned on the card. How wonderful, how sublimely thoughtful!

Next morning, we all went into the woods. Braving the slippery bridge, helping each other to cross it, we found that the food laid out for the rabbits was now for a great deal eaten up. The rabbits had come back. A miracle? Most assuredly!

6

Excerpts from a Diary

Five days after our return to Australia, our friends Mike, Margaret and Giles arrived. Margaret, by the way is Mike's wife, and Giles his brother. They also came from the little country in Europe, and their visit was meant to explore the possibilities of emigration. Their stay was, we thought, very pleasant and certainly fruitful. Furthermore, they also belonged to what I described in the preceding chapters as 'The Centre', and so it needs no lengthy explanation to describe their understanding of nature-spirits.

Bor soon told them about Dhawana, and on the following day, when they went out for a drive around the neighbourhood, they very soon finished up at

Dhawana's in National Park. I stayed home making dinner and, of course, I came to hear all about it after their return home.

Now Mike is a very meticulous person, and he used to write down every detail of what happened during their trip. Therefore, I thought it a good idea to quote his version of what they experienced in connection with Dhawana. They forwarded it to us by way of a letter after their return home, and here then is Mike's contribution:

"A part of yesterday's activities consisted of Bor taking us over to National Park, where we stopped at a certain place and told us that here Roma and himself had unexpectedly come in contact with a nature-spirit called Dhawana. This nature-spirit lives in the Park, and his assistants are very small, approximately fifty to sixty centimetres tall. At this self-same spot are also erected several etherical buildings, (in fact, there was only one – Roma) as Bor explained to us. When he took us up to this particular place, all of us felt definitely something to be there. Margaret even got goosepimples all over — at 39°C! Giles felt as if being far and deep into the woods, a feeling of utter serenity.

I felt something indefinable after being approximately ten paces away from the car. Bor then introduced the three of us to Dhawana, and he conveyed warm greetings from Parma as he had promised to do. Through this introduction, something inconceivable seemed to take place in us. First, Dhawana was standing in front of us, but very soon it seemed as if all four of us were being encircled by this wonderful being. A wonderfully fine experience."

So far, for their first encounter with Dhawana, we too had always experienced this as something very special and we were not in the least surprised about their reaction. About one week later, we decided to pay Dhawana another visit. This time I also joined the party. And once more, here follows Mike's account:

"When we arrived at the spot in National Park, Dhawana was not to be seen. And he did not turn up either. But at a certain moment, Roma apparently seemed to detect something. Without any warning she walked off, trying to climb a steep, gravelled hill, sometimes on hands and knees. Bor, after some hesitation, followed her in order to assist her, and together they disappeared into the bush. After some time, they returned, and Roma was very distressed. She told us she had seen a glimpse of Dhawana, just on the other side of the hill, and that was why she had acted so impetuously. She had found him standing next to a tree, obviously angry, or at least very perturbed. He even stamped his foot when asked what ailed him, and it took considerable time to extract from him the reason for his peculiar attitude. At last, however, he calmed down a little, and bit by bit, the story came out. It appeared he had received word that his leading role at the Park was shortly to be terminated and that someone else was to take over. For such a long, long time he had dwelt in this place and now he must hand it over to someone else. Roma was so sorrowful about it, thinking this to be a final farewell from Dhawana. The picture his words had conjured up indeed made us sad, and we did not know what to do. Until we found a solution. 'Would you like to come and live with us, Dhawana?' we sent out to him. That made Dhawana happy, and us too, for that matter."

How we were going to contrive this was something we did not, as yet, know. But we did not let this bother us. The future would show what had to be done, we thought. The main thing was that Dhawana was back on his feet again, knowing us to be his friends, whatever happened. Margaret had to return home earlier than her husband and Giles, because of her three children. She had seen what she wanted to see in Australia, and so we took her to the airport and said farewell. After that, Mike and Giles went for a trip south and when they returned, on their request, we once again went to see Dhawana. Here again is Mike's account, the last one of their stay with us:

"Roma told us in the car on our way to Dhawana what he looked like. Very big, enormously strong, and black. His helpers are much smaller, having the appearance of little human beings, little males and females. Their task is to maintain balance in the woods. But Dhawana reigns uppermost in National Park. We went to the usual place, but he was definitely not there. Roma said he was sometimes to be found by the waterfall. So, we all went to the falls in the car where it was bustling with people. We searched for a secluded spot and there we sat ourselves down. Soon Dhawana appeared on the opposite side of the stream, standing close to a tree. He told us he was enchanted by the idea of coming to live with us, although he was rather concerned at imposing too much on us. This certainly is not the case. Roma asked him what his thoughts were about the large piece of land in Highmeadows we had seen, and on which we could eventually build our houses. He scratched his head and said: 'Six months is too long, in about two months' time someone else is to take my place.' (What did he mean by "six months?") He said he could easily go to a friend of his, but this was far away, and he did not like it. He thought it wonderful for all of us to join up forces, but it was better to wait and see what the future had in store. He asked Bor and Roma whether they would take him over there one day in order to see for himself. The only help he could offer momentarily was to keep others from buying it. That was all — very little I must admit — but out of little things something big could arise. After that, he seemed to be in a hurry to leave. With Roma's help I could just contrive to ask him a question: 'Would it be possible to contact him from our country in Europe?' This posed no problem, he said. Thoughts could travel all over the world and even through the Cosmos. Then he was gone. It obviously seems to be a great effort on his part to materialise himself in order to make himself visible. That was actually the reason why he had us come to the waterfall, because water seems to intensify the process. Never before had he conversed with Bor and Roma for such a long time. Soon after that, we went home for lunch and then we left for the airport. Our visit to Australia had come to an end."

7

Intermezzo

Later in the month we contacted Dhawana again and made an appointment to explore the land in Highmeadows we had in mind to buy. It had posed a bit of a problem in our minds, for how were we to transport our dear Dhawana to this place? Take him with us in the car? We thought this rather odd. But we should not have troubled ourselves with it.

"I'll be there," Dhawana said as if it was the simplest thing in the world.

It was a beautiful Sunday morning when we set out for our new adventure, and at the appointed time we arrived at our destination. Beforehand, we had collected the key for the gate to the property, and soon we rambled over the paths criss-crossing it.

About half-way, I asked Bor to please stop the car. A little away from where we were standing was a clump of trees, some fair-sized rocks scattered around underneath. I thought I had seen some movement there, and so we set off for the place I indicated to Bor. And there, sitting comfortably on one of the rocks, was Dhawana, welcoming us with one of his warm, broad smiles.

We felt a little at a disadvantage with all our complicated contraptions: using a motor-car to reach this place, taking folding chairs to sit on, having prepared and taken lunch. But soon we were all at ease, for we simply had to resign to the fact that this belonged to our way of living, and the other things to the life of a nature-spirit. So we sat ourselves down on the other side of the clump of trees, and rapidly, an unusual feeling of extreme happiness seemed to come over us. Bor looked at me, I looked at him, and together we looked at Dhawana. What could be the meaning of this, we thought, although we did not put this into words.

"I'll tell you," Dhawana said after he had given us time to let this feeling penetrate our entire being.

"Have you ever thought about the meaning of my name? We nature-spirits never carry a meaningless name, you know, and I'm happy to tell you now that my name, Dhawana, stands for 'BE HAPPY' in our language."

How wonderful! Could there be any name more charming than this? We laughed, for this feeling of happiness was of an extraordinary quality. For some time, we talked about it with Dhawana. It was a subject containing many facets. For instance, his moment of unhappiness in National Park not so long ago. But Dhawana told us that it was all meant for the good. For eight hundred years now, he said, he had lived in the Park (which, naturally, had been wild bush in the beginning,) And, coming to think of it, it was actually high time for a change. Dhawana, after having contemplated the whole thing for some time, had come to the conclusion that he was gaining tremendously by it: adventure, moving to different places, getting to know more about other things, people, in fact an endless array of possibilities. And shouldn't he be happy about it? Certainly, it would be very ungrateful not to see it in that light.

Then he told us about the spot where we were sitting at this particular moment. It was an old ceremonial place, long ago used by Aboriginal people — the original inhabitants of Australia. They had called this place: 'Sacred Hill', Dhawana explained, and the ceremonies which took place there were meant to commemorate happy events. What a wonderful idea, we thought. Why don't we do that too. Why do we always commemorate sad, unhappy things like war, and all those sort of morbid events? And here they were: the most simple living people, so far advanced that they took it upon themselves to come together and commemorate and celebrate the happy events of life. And by doing so, they were happy all over again.

'Sacred Hill' at the seventy-acre land

It was a quiet and beautiful morning we spent there with Dhawana. But at last, we had to go. At the point of saying farewell, Dhawana invited us to visit him again at the old place in National Park. In the car, on the way home, we suddenly realized that Dhawana had categorically avoided talking either about the terrain, nor about the possibilities of all of us living there together. And we wondered what the reason behind it could be.

A few days later, we obediently went to National Park again. When we arrived at what was by now firmly established in our minds as 'Dhawana's', something unusual took place. Come to think of it now, I realize that every single time, unexpected and unusual things happened. No two meetings have ever been similar to each other. It was never dull, never uninteresting. And this time as well, it differed again from every preceding encounter. Bor and I had set ourselves quietly on the ground, waiting for Dhawana, as he had requested. His favoured spot, however, next to the cork-screwed tree, remained empty, although we had informed him of our coming. We had experienced Dhawana not being there before, therefore it did not disturb us very much. This time he had invited us, so it would certainly turn out all right.

Bor and I talked a little together, but then we became very quiet. For some time, we sat there, motionless. Then it happened. A little to the left of the cork-screwed tree, seen from our point of view, something hazy came into being. First almost invisible, but slowly developing into something more tangible. To our utter amazement, after some time, I saw it taking on a form, first unrecognizable, shapeless, but then it began to dawn on me that it was shaping itself into a being... Dhawana! How we laughed, and Dhawana laughed with us. What an unusual occasion, for never before had he put on such a performance for us. Dhawana laughed again, but although we tried hard, we could not get a word out of him. He stood there with his usual broad smile on his face, waiting as it seemed for something else to happen. So we kept very, very quiet, also waiting, but not knowing what we were waiting for. Then, suddenly, the same thing happened as before. To Dhawana's right another hazy something appeared. And slowly this also materialised, took on more shape, and at last appeared before our eyes as a separate and different entity. To the best of my ability, I shall try to give a description of it, although I know that words would never be capable of giving the right impression. It was not by any means a duplicate of Dhawana. I noticed immediately that it stood for a female being, although I wonder whether in the case of nature-spirits male and female is of so much importance as it is to us. However, as this being was wearing a lightly flowing dress, a flower in her almost fair hair, it was strongly recognizable as a female. Another thing which amazed us was that she was much smaller than Dhawana. Her colouring also appeared to be much lighter, a different nature-spirit altogether. Besides, Dhawana, I should also mention, was much more solidly constructed than she was, she being more etherical than he. At last — although I must say everything took place much faster than I can describe it — Dhawana spoke.

"May I introduce you to my successor?" he said. "Her name is Semborah, and although I originally regretted the course of events, I must be honest with you in saying that Semborah and I have become good friends. She is very capable and is learning fast in connection with the requirements of our park. Everything will turn out splendidly, you'll see."

If ever we had expected anything, it certainly was not this! The very idea of a woman placed in such a demanding position was a thought which would never have entered our minds. It just shows how smallminded we human beings still are. 'Dhawana: Be Happy'. Is this in actual fact not the crux of the whole matter? We left, richer than we had come, humbler too. We had learned another lesson on the path that leads to more knowledge and more understanding.

8

THE MESSAGE

"I'm going to take you out," said Bor resolutely.

I looked a little doubtful, for I had been rather ill lately; as a matter of fact, for several months, and suddenly going out was a bit much, I thought. But it was a beautiful winter's day, the sun was shining and going for a drive through National Park was perhaps more of a cure than anything else. It seemed ages since we had been to Dhawana's special spot, and so it was high time to go and see how things stood. It was extremely quiet in the park on this mid-week afternoon. No cars, and no people. The wildflowers were already beginning to show some foretaste of what would be an abundance of nature's beauty in the months to come. How lovely and peaceful it was. And even more so when a kangaroo suddenly came hopping over the road, just in front of us, and entering the bush on the opposite side, joining two of his friends who were already there. Bor immediately stopped the car and surprisingly the 'three clowns of the forests' stopped still on their hind legs, their two little front legs protruding in their own inimitable funny way and looking curiously at this nonsensical piece of metal on the road. Expecting them to disappear quickly into the bush, we couldn't believe our eyes when they showed no signs of doing so. They kept on staring at us, not unlike Parma and his friends last year. But at long last, we decided to continue along the road and leave them to their own devices. Nevertheless, it was something never to be forgotten.

We parked the car at the old familiar spot and walked the short distance to Dhawana's headquarters. As I was not yet completely recovered from my recent illness, I was out of breath, so Bor suggested we should sit down at the edge of the hollow, which we did. It was so quiet and serene in the bush, and soon we were in perfect harmony with everything around us.

Naturally our eyes wandered over the scene in order to try catching a glimpse of Dhawana or one of his helpers. But there was absolutely nothing. As was usually the case, my concentration became deeper and then it became very clear that the place was deserted, and had been so for some time.

"Well," Bor said, "that's nice. What are we going to do now? Dhawana and all the rest lost to us? It will be an impossible task in this vast land to go and search for him."

At that moment, we heard the sound of wings moving through the air, right behind us. We looked up, for never before had we seen any birds so close by at this particular place. But we left it at that and continued with our conversation. Though not for long. To our utter amazement, three beautiful magpies, their feathers shining like polished black and white marble, their glittering eyes focussed on the two invaders sitting there on the ground, approached us without any fear. Elegantly lifting their delicate legs, their heads scrutinizingly turned to one side, now and then bringing forth the most endearing little sounds, they paraded in front of, and all around us. We wondered whether this could be a message coming from Dhawana, but although we listened carefully to their sounds, we could make neither head nor tail of it. One thing however it had brought about: it had focussed our eyes more or less for some time to the ground, and suddenly I felt myself attracted towards a piece of rock laying in front of us. I immediately put the thought of it aside, but time and again, it seemed as if it lured me back to it, until at last I mentioned this queer feeling to Bor. Both of us came to the same conclusion, namely that the stone had not been there before, as we had sat at this selfsame spot many a time. Bor got up and picked up the stone.

"Hold it in your hand," he said. "Stones can often tell you something."

By now, I was already fairly convinced that this piece of rock was left there for us, and when I took it carefully into my hands, I was quite sure about it.

"Let's see whether the stone tells us something by its outward appearance," I suggested.

It was easy to see that a piece had recently been broken off, as the edges were still fresh and sharp.

"Yes," we said. "So Dhawana must feel himself to be. But why? Nature-spirits do not hurt each other. What then could be the reason?"

Part of the stone was touched by fire and this could, maybe, contain the answer to our questions: Dhawana too, like everyone else, had 'to go through fire' in order to evolutionize. Stupid as it may seem, that was about all we were able to achieve from the stone's exterior. Bor, by now becoming rather curious, found it imperative to get to the core of the matter. I therefore enclosed the stone with both hands and yes, there it was, Dhawana's message, as clear as a bell. How glorious, we thought, how absolutely marvellous is everything created by God. If man only knew and wanted to discover for himself, what a different world we could be living in! And this is what Dhawana's message consisted of:

"This is no longer our meeting place. Momentarily, I am scouting around, but do not let me give you the impression that I am unhappy. I am on the friendliest of terms with Semborah, and everything is working out better than I expected. Nevertheless, we all have to go through experiences like the piece of rock you recognized so well as being placed there by me for you to find. Sometimes we get a little battered like the stone, or brandished by fire, though finally it is all for the good. But also like the stone you are holding in your hands — because that is the only way to receive my message — our friendship with you, people, is indissoluble, so there you are. Let us give ourselves over to the stream of life, meanwhile not forgetting to see to it that the ship carrying us must be kept well on course. And being in harmony with nature and all of God's creations is of all things the most important."

How well we understood, first of all, why we found the place deserted. A new leader of the Park, new ideas to be brought in, newly designed places to be installed. Oh yes, no doubt all this was so obviously logical. And furthermore, the start of Dhawana's new life could not happen all at once, although we ourselves had so many unanswered questions. Anyhow, there certainly is a time for everything. Needless to say, we took the stone with us, and there it is, together with our collection of other precious stones, for we think they are the most fascinating things in the world.

9

WHERE IS DHAWANA?

Now a time full of uncertainties was to follow. Months went by, and not much opportunity presented itself for going out and trying to contact our dear friend, Dhawana. Several times I endeavoured to reach him mentally, but all I could report to Bor was that I felt him to be far away. Once or twice, we drove through National Park, but no Dhawana was to be seen or felt. We also felt very unsure about the land we had in mind to buy in Highmeadows, in conjunction with Mike, Margaret and Giles, for although they went on with the proceedings concerning their emigration, nothing definite emerged.

Meanwhile, Bor and I kept on searching for various possibilities in the same area, but it all came to nothing. Furthermore, we did not feel very happy with our explorations there either, so we left it more or less for time to decide what was to be done. Nothing really seemed to be working[1]. The time for our yearly trip to Europe was drawing nearer and nearer. The flight had been booked, and the tickets were in our possession. We were trying to find people to live in our house for the three months we would be away. This didn't work either. Deep within, a feeling of uneasiness grew stronger and stronger, and at last we had to face facts. After the long illness I had experienced this year, I wasn't at all up to an enterprise like that. So we tried to change things a little, postponing our trip to some five weeks later. Then one sunny day (by the way, most days are sunny in Australia!), Bor suggested making a trip to a small place at the seaside called Chanyup, some seventy-five kilometres from where we were living. It was a lovely little village, quiet, with beautiful beaches, rocks, caves, dunes and a cute little harbour with sailing boats. Before entering the road leading up to this, there even was another National Park, although much smaller than 'our' National Park. Different too. A lovely lake with black swans, pelicans and ducks. A protected section with kangaroos and koala bears, all in all, immensely charming. When we arrived in Chanyup, we first paid a visit to a long-standing friend of our son Maurice, who owns a pottery-cum-gallery there. We fell in love with Chanyup in the most inconceivable way. And the long and the short of it was that this self-same day we decided to buy a dear little beach-house there.

The beach house at Chanyup

The view from the house was beautiful, the ever-blue sea at some two minutes' walking distance, a never-ending delight. Right in front of us was a funny-looking high dune, absolutely out of proportion with all the rest. We had to pass it to reach the beach, and the first time we sat in our chairs along the water's edge, I suddenly felt something peculiar happening. No doubt it came from behind us, but when I rather abruptly turned around, there was nothing to be seen, neither on the beach, nor at the sand-hill. I left it at that, but the feeling returned, even stronger than before. Then I knew: Dhawana!

"He's here, Dhawana!" I called out to Bor, too surprised to keep my voice down. "Can you imagine, here of all things!"

How happy we both were. This beautiful, unspoilt terrain, so big, so open, and transmitting such a happy atmosphere. We couldn't have wished for any better for Dhawana. We now realized how degrading it would have been for him to live with us in such a restricted way in Highmeadows, even on a seventy-acre piece of land, compared to what he was used to. This, yes, this was an enormous improvement, no doubt about that. Sitting there on the beach that day, I could strongly feel his joy. I could feel him transmitting the glory of his freedom. And... yes! His pride in having induced us to buy this house in Chanyup without us even dreaming he was motivating!

After some four weeks, the house became available to us, and ready to receive us, because that's what it really did. No wonder we baptised it immediately 'DHAWANA', and on Christmas morning Maurice surprised us with a beautiful signboard which he had painted, carrying Dhawana's name, which was bolted on to the house at once.

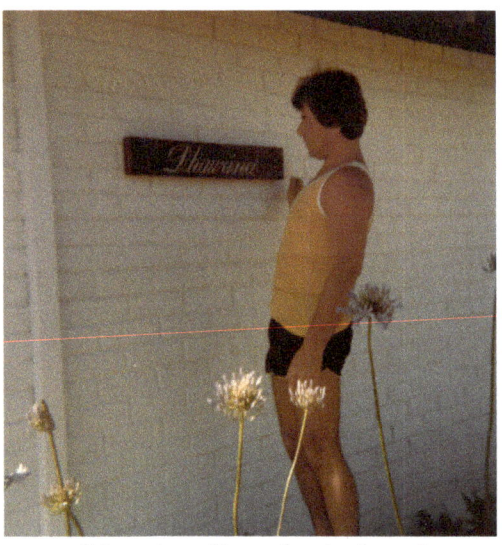

Maurice adjusts the signboard
'DHAWANA' on the wall of the beach house

Meanwhile, we were at different times contacted by Dhawana. We knew him to be pacing unrestrictedly over his new domain, saying to himself time and time again:

"I'm so happy, so happy… I'm free… free, free…!"

Then, after some weeks, he came to tell us about his adventures since the time he left National Park, and I did my utmost to put his narrative on paper, although his monologue was so rapid, I nearly stumbled over my own pen. So, the following two chapters are fully Dhawana's, and I leave you to him, hoping you'll enjoy his jolly rendition of what happened to him during the time our contact with him had somewhat slackened.

---

1. Actually, the plan never eventuated.

10

Dhawana's Narration

"It's about time to come together and make up for the months that lie behind. There is so much to be told, so much to unravel. Where shall I begin? Yes, without a doubt in National Park. Whenever I look back to that I feel so ashamed. Never during all those long, long years did I lose myself so completely as at that one afternoon when you caught me at my lowest point. Defeated, I felt, humiliated, and I don't know what else. My living ground, all my 'subjects' as I used to call them, the work I had done. Brushed aside, yes, I think that was the worst. How stupid this was. But I first had to learn it the hard way. (What do you say, don't we all learn the hard way?) Anyhow, I won't whine about it anymore. Several events you have already encountered. Semborah, for instance. What courage to take on a job like that. I wouldn't have it returned to me for all the gold in Kalgoorlie. What good would it do me anyway!

Now, do you recall that specific time? You, all of you, so kindly offered to come and share your lives. It delighted me, no; it warmed my heart in no uncertain way. I'll never be able to tell you how much. Thank you ...

Then came the time of uncertainty: would Margaret, Mike and Giles be able to come to Australia; your long illness, Roma; the land you wanted to buy; etc., etc. Yes, I said to myself, it's a nice piece of land, and I must go and live there. I'll go and live there. That's something I shall have to learn, I thought. Humbleness is not my strongest point, I thought, so I consented to it right there and then on that beautiful Sunday morning, sitting at Sacred Hill with you two. My sacrifice, do you understand? Afterward I talked strongly and sternly to my bleeding heart, for my beautiful Park was still such a living part of myself. Then the time arrived when I had to hand out all the assistance I could give to Semborah. And bit by bit, more and more, I discovered what a rather boring and unadventurous life I had led during all those endless years. And I felt actually sorry for dear little Semborah, although she seemed to enjoy everything to the full. I must explain that she is in fact the first female ever to hold a post like that on earth. A real swing in nature-spirits' history. What-ho, take note of that, my friends!

Slowly it penetrated my being — and was it ever so slow! — that at the disclosure of my dismissal the following message had been added to it:

'Now you'll be free to go wherever you choose to, Dhawana.'

But did I care? Did I want it? No Sir, not me. Ugh, I was like a child, feeling so sorry for myself. Remember me saying to you:

"I could go to a friend of mine, but that is so far away." Far away, what is far away? Well, one day feeling somewhat happier than before, and slowly realising I was no longer tied up to anything, I thought to myself, oh what, why not go and see my friend so far away? So I sent him word of my coming and off I went, roaming here and roaming there, feeling more relaxed than I had for ages. Do you know why I had hesitated for so long? I must confess this to you, for I trust you, you see. He, my friend, was, lo-and-behold, also an appointed leader over another National Park. Not as big as mine had been, but still, I was parkless, as you might say. And wouldn't I be a little, just a little jealous when I met him again? His name is Broyah, and until about a hundred and fifty years ago, he had been a subject, a pupil of mine. A good one, a clever one, oh yes, but can't you see? I, jobless, he, a settled somebody.

'Oh Dhawana,' I thought whilst I was roaming around, 'Oh Dhawana, what are you doing to yourself?' Dhawana: Be happy! Goodness me, was I forgetting whom I was? 'You're quite mad,' I said to myself, and I laughed and laughed until I had thrown off all my silly petty feelings and found my own self again, but this time more purified by the flames of the fire I had gone through."

11

Dhawana Continues

"I had a wonderful time with my friend Broyah in the Park. More carefree, more joyful than I had ever experienced before. Broyah did his utmost to make my stay with him pleasant. He took me to the section where the kangaroos and koala bears lived, and explained to me that their captive life was inevitable in order to save them from extinction. And the good animals conveyed to me that they were quite happy as they were, although some criminal minds had lately seen fit to destroy several of their community. Broyah and I also walked along the lake, but mostly after sundown when all was quiet. For I must confess that I have a great weakness: I am afraid of water! And now see the irony of the Creator's plan, for our lives are always part of that plan, you see...

Sitting quietly one night under Broyah's favoured tree at the spot where he had his headquarters, he suddenly very seriously turned to me.

"Listen Dhawana," he said. "I would like to talk to you about yourself and your future life. I know you are free to go wherever you want to. So far, how do you like it?"

"Oh," I said rather surprised, "fine, I think, I mean I haven't spent much thought on my future life yet. I enjoy moving around over places I've never been to before. I'm free, free... That's a wonderful experience, Broyah."

"Oh," said Broyah.

"What do you mean 'oh'? Is that all you want to say?"

"No," said Broyah.

"Oh, come on, speak up man, out with it. We nature-spirits never have any secrets from each other, you know that."

Broyah laughed. "All right. But it suddenly struck me how much freedom means to you, Dhawana.

And I wouldn't dream of interfering with it. Though I'll tell you what I actually had in mind. Perhaps, I don't know, a little grain of selfishness is unwittingly entwined with it."

"You never were, and you'll never be a selfish creature, Broyah. So don't talk nonsense."

"Well..." and he still appeared to be hesitant. "Well, it is like this, Dhawana. Past our National Park here, just where the road branches off to the west, lies a terrain which still is, you might say, in a primary state of human development. Its acreage is big, far bigger than your former territory. Undulating terrain, with the Indian Ocean all along the west side. Human beings have begun settling there, building their houses, and things going together with their ways of living, like a harbour and boats, playgrounds, schools, industries, and what not, although the greatest part is still in its natural state. I would like you to go there and inspect it."

In the greatest amazement, I listened to what he was saying. For a moment, I was silent. Then: "Do you want to tell me..." I said, trying to compose myself a little. "The Ocean? A harbour? Boats? I've heard of the sea, it is I believe a big, vast quantity of water. Man, do you think I'm not well in my upperworks? Thank you very much, Broyah, you mean well, but no, thank you."

"I'm sorry, Dhawana, I didn't want to... I only wanted you to have a look around this terrain. No more, I am so sorry..."

He looked so sad, and suddenly I felt sorry too. I didn't want to hurt him, most certainly not. You see, our whole being is made up of feelings, of emotions. Perhaps I could say: your emotional is our physical. Do you understand? And therefore, feelings, like joy, happiness, sorrow, anger, fear, etc., are of the utmost importance to us. It is our life's task to try to master them all. How else could we be of any help to everything in nature?

Therefore, I said to Broyah: "Ah well, what could it do to me, just looking around, if it gives you pleasure?"

Broyah did not answer me, but he looked so happy. And that in itself was already sufficient reason for me to at least give it a try.

The next day, I set out on my journey. I had no trouble finding my way. In actual fact, our 'instinct', as you might call it, guides us always safely to where we want to go, even when we've never been there before. That day I walked through a section very similar to Broyah's Park. And suddenly something struck me so forcibly that I decided to go back to my good friend and ask him a most important question, a question I completely forgot the day before. I stood still, ready to inform him telepathically of my intention to return, when his own message reached me at the same time.

"Yes Dhawana, of course you'll find nature-spirits there. But there's no need to come back to me. You say that they look at you without any interest? You see, you're only a passing visitor, aren't you? And they don't know what to do, because you're so big. Why not approach them from your side? Humbleness has never been a vice, didn't you tell me so, long ago?"

I felt ashamed. Yes, I had seen some nature-spirits. But as they did not seem to have any intention of approaching me, I actually had avoided them more than they had done themselves. So I searched for a hollow place and sat myself down to think it all over. Freedom certainly has its advantages, but it also poses uncertainties.

The following day found me walking through almost the same kind of territory, although the vegetation started to thin out. I wondered about the nature-spirits I saw here and there peeping at me. They were a different-looking species, different to those I had experienced before, even at Broyah's. Those must be sand-spirits, or maybe they are called dune-spirits, I thought.

'Why don't you go and ask them?' I clearly heard Broyah send out to me. He certainly seemed to keep an eye on me! I laughed, more relaxed now that I knew I was not completely left alone.

But no, I felt, I need more time, it's still too early. And I suddenly realised that I hadn't gone far either. Deep within, I knew why this was actually so. The Ocean.

Yes, I was purposefully trying to postpone facing up to it. And discovering my cowardice brought about just the opposite: in the shortest of time, I covered more ground than I did since leaving Broyah. I met with all sorts of things: dunes, roads, houses. 'Yes,' I told myself, 'you cannot avoid that, for you knew about it, Dhawana!' Even a small airfield with little aeroplanes, which fascinated me. But then it was there, my goodness, some water! Ugh! I stood still, like a pillar of stone!

"All right Dhawana," I said, "face it man, do not close your eyes."

Oh yes, that sounded brave enough, but somewhere in my great big toe, there still was that teasing tinkling of fear. It's no good, I thought. What to do about it?

"Can I help?" I suddenly heard someone saying next to me. I had to bend down in order to see who it was. To my great surprise, I saw a little nature-spirit, but so different to what I had been used to, that I said in an unbelieving voice:

"What... Who are you?"

"I'm a sea-spirit, and my name is Whindy... Can I help?"

"Whindy... hello... My name is Dhawana."

"Oh, I know that; we knew you were coming... Welcome Dhawana. Can I help?"

Now, you know, how could I, big burly me, bring myself to confess to this lovely little thing that I was afraid of the sea? This suddenly took away the last bit of fear still left over in my great big toe. And laughingly I said:

"You've helped me already. How did you happen to come here? Weren't you afraid of a big monster like me?"

"Well," she confessed, "to tell you the truth, I was, but only in the outer part of my left flipper. And that's gone now, after you laughed so kindly to me."

Now we both laughed, and I felt happier than I had done for a long time. But first, I better describe the dear little creature to you. Blue like the sea, and wafty, yes, wafty is the right word for it. All sorts of pastel blue colours were constantly wafting through her being. A finely chiselled face, so kind, also so full of fun. And her feet, which she called 'flippers', were actually more or less waftying things. Then you saw them, then you didn't. Charming, absolutely char ming."

12

BACK AGAIN IN EUROPE

This time it took a little longer getting used to the cold, after having experienced several weeks of over 40°C in Australia. But one morning we thought ourselves fit enough to brave the weather and wrapped up in warm clothes, we set out for a walk in the woods. The ground was still somewhat frozen, and the fallen leaves crackled under our feet. All in all, nature showed itself from a rather crispy and invigorating side. As usual, we stopped at the old place in front of the bridge. But although we felt no objections coming from the other side and were therefore free to do as we wanted, the chief impression we received was that no one was waiting for us. Soon we understood. During the previous weeks, the moat and brooks had been solidly frozen over, and a lot of skating had been going on. That's the time when there are no boundaries, when all waterways are everybody's property — and why not? And thus you see people wherever they can exercise their sport. Now, finding a little bridge obstructing their path, they had to climb over it, and fragile as the thing already was, it seemed no great wonder that it partly collapsed under the strain. With some acrobatic efforts, it still wouldn't pose a problem, but we decided not to force the issue, and so we turned the other way, as there was still another entrance. Katie had given us the key of the gate, knowing the bridge to be in such a state, so we walked the distance to the other side of the wood, where Bor unlocked the gate and we entered the wood over another bridge, which we had never done before.

BACK AGAIN IN EUROPE

Bor opening the gate to the other entrance to the wood

Knowing we had Parma's consent, we turned to the right into the forest-lane with its majestic looking rows of beech-trees bordering it on both sides. We knew this lane to be leading up to the other side of the little bridge, and we enjoyed to the full the silent beauty of everything around us. We continued on our way until we reached a spot about halfway along the path, from where we could see the other end, when I saw some movement there, next to one of the big trees. I asked Bor to stand still and yes, there he was, Parma, together with some of his helpers. Enthusiastically, he waved with his funny little hat, and of course we waved back, Bor even taking off his own cap and using it as a token of our own enthusiasm. Then, from under the shrubs, more of the little people emerged, and to our amazement, they started to dance and sing. Now, how in heaven's name can I describe this? In actual fact I cannot, but I'll endeavour to do it to the best of my ability, although I know that the result will be very poor. Their dancing was, naturally, very joyful, mainly consisting of little leaps into the air, and very humorous to watch. But their singing! I've never heard anything like it, and if ever I thought myself able to notate in music whatever I heard, this time I felt incapable and defeated, to say the least. Do you know what I would like to do? Fill up this page with little dots. That's how the little people's singing was! Little tones, high, clear, leaping through the air, just like their happy dancing. No connection, no melodic lines, only dots, beautiful bell-like dots, that's the best way to describe it. So enchanting, so natural, so completely at ease.

The forest lane where the nature-spirits danced and sang

After a little while — for these sorts of performances never seem to last for long — it abruptly stopped. Parma then drew himself up in front of his friends, who formed themselves into line behind him, and gesticulating to us to follow them, the whole group took off, deeper into the wood, to the spot where we had seen them for the very first time. We followed them for a while, but the speed with which they moved was too high for us, so we stopped and said we would go back. Then Parma stopped as well, and from afar he sent out the following message to us, after we still found a chance to send him the somewhat belated greetings from Dhawana.

"Thank you," said Parma, "and tell Dhawana that here, as well, changeable times are at hand. Forces stronger than ours will supplement our ranks, reinforcements necessary to infiltrate our environment, in order to be able to generate more and stronger forces for the world itself, and for all living creatures around us. You'll say, it's only a small contribution, but we know that this principle is being exercised wherever possible. Please, do tell Dhawana, I'm sure it will make him happy to know that he's not alone."

Naturally, we promised Parma we would fulfil this task, and then said goodbye to our dear friends in the wood. But this wasn't enough.

"Oh, by the way," said Parma, "the rabbits are begging for a special favour. They would like you to convey their special greetings to the rabbits in Australia, and above all, to the rabbits in Dhawana's territory."

With a smile, we promised to do this as well, very well knowing that we couldn't by any means reach all the rabbits of Australia. But we found it a charming thought and after kindly taking leave of Parma and his friends, we went back along the same beech-bordered lane. On our left was the stream, covered in ice. In the middle of the stream was a little tree-clad island. Almost having passed it, I felt something to be there. I asked Bor to stand still again, but looking intently at the island, I couldn't see anything. However, from there a strong feeling reached us: it clearly appeared to be the dwelling-place of the gnome-family, the four little friends of our first encounter, the guardians of the bridge. This was a nice and unexpected end to our enterprise of that particular day. Happily, we passed through and closed the gate and after our arrival home, we told Katie of our last adventure in the wood. Later on, we would also tell Dhawana about it, and we were sure he would appreciate hearing from his unknown friends in the far-away country.

The little island where the gnome family lives

13

Dhawana's New Life

"No wonder you didn't see them," Dhawana said. "They are much farther out at sea."

Bor and I had been sitting along the water's edge on the beach at Chanyup, listening to the sound of the waves, seeing them continuously moving along, one after another, never stopping. As it was so quiet and the sea so blue, we pondered over what Dhawana had told us about the sea-spirits. Wouldn't this be an ideal opportunity for seeing them, riding the waves, playing together, happily living their joyous lives? I brought myself into a state of complete relaxation, wiping all thoughts from my mind, open to those wonderful workings of nature. But to no avail.

"No wonder…" Dhawana said from afar, after we had arrived home.

It was already the second weekend after we had returned from our European trip. Eager to see Dhawana, wanting to hear what had happened to him in the meantime, and to tell him about our adventures in the woods with Parma. But Dhawana was not to be found. We felt very disappointed, Bor, Maurice and I, and we could not understand what was going on. Therefore, we had to exercise patience, lots of it, especially as we couldn't see any reason for it. But now, at last he granted us this one meagre sentence, though 'telegraphed' from another place, and we had to be content with that.

Today, however, sitting on the terrace of our home in the hills, I strongly felt Dhawana trying to contact us. I quickly went for my writing pad, in case I had to jot something down. This proved to be a proper decision, for I heard Dhawana clearly start talking:

"You must have thought me very uncivil," he said. "Not welcoming you after your trip overseas, not transmitting any message to you, not even appearing for a single moment on the hill opposite your beach house, the hill you three so kindly named after me: 'MOUNT DHAWANA'. I still want to thank you for that, as well as for the baptizing of your house, what a wonderful thought."

"Was a pleasure, Dhawana, we wouldn't have done otherwise. But do tell me what happened? You haven't been ill, have you, for I don't think nature-spirits can ever be ill?"

"No... no... Though I'm still in hospital..."

"What? Dhawana, you give me a fright. What's the matter?"

"Oh, don't get upset. I'll tell you all about it, and when you've heard everything, you'll find it probably rather funny. Well now, where were we last time we communicated? Ah, I know: I had met Whindy. That was the beginning of it all. Hm... it seems so long ago... meanwhile so much has happened. Anyhow, she asked me to follow her, and so I did. After some time, we came to a place where some rock formations stood along the beach. No, not at the spot where you mostly draw yourselves up when going to the beach, but to a much more secluded spot. There, to my great astonishment, a large group of nature-spirits awaited me: sand-, or I should rather say dune-spirits, shrub-spirits, flower-spirits and sea-spirits, all together in one great, big gathering. I closed my eyes, found it too overwhelming, felt shy, and clumsy and what not, and got possessed by only one wish: run away, Dhawana, run away. But when I opened my eyes, I saw them radiating friendliness, I felt their love, their happiness, and I was pretty well ashamed of myself. Now, the thing that struck me most, was that they were all so delicate, so finely chiselled, I would say. And I felt more clumsy than ever. Anyhow, there was not much time to pay sufficient attention to this particular problem, for soon a most extraordinary thing happened. I could not believe my ears — yes, my ears, mind you — for they suddenly started to serenade me! Oh, it was lovely. So serene, so unusual because, as they were representatives of different species, their voices also were of diverse qualities, and the resulting effect was simply unforgettable. When everything was over, a feeling of warmth had crept into my entire being.

With an almost broken voice I thanked them, and I saw the happiness on their faces.

"Dhawana!" they ejaculated in chorus. "Be happy!" They knew what it meant and boy, did I feel happy!

Then one of the shrub-spirits came forward, and suddenly all fell silent. He was an impressive looking fellow, clad in a solid looking brownish sort of tunic, a green trunk-hose, and top-boots. A short-clipped little sailor's beard adorned his face, and his hair looked like a mop on a stormy day.

'Now I'm in for something,' I thought, 'for after all, I'm an intruder here.'

He appeared to be a person of few words.

"Would you like to be our leader?" he said. "We never had a real one, and it's about time we got one." Then, without any scruples, he immediately continued: "We hereby proclaim you to be our chief."

"Hi!" I yelled in utter distress. "Wait a minute, I can't. Don't you understand? I do not know you, I have no experience with your kind of living conditions, with this kind of terrain, I'm afraid of water and..." Here my voice dropped considerably. "I am far, far too big."

A cacophony of voices arose in answer to my stammered speech. "We'll help you!" they shouted.

"All those things can be rectified!"

"Give it a go..."

"It only takes time..."

On and on they went. They formed a circle around me, looking at me with so much trust that I didn't know what to do. At last, I threw up my hands.

"My dear, dear people," I said. "I'm overwhelmed and honoured. I would like to give it a try, but honestly, I think I'll be a failure. See how clumsy I am... really..."

There was not a chance in the world for me to go any further. They danced around me, they laughed, they called out all sorts of encouragements. They even told me I could get used to the water. But no, I'll save that story for later."

Here Dhawana stopped talking. And I, having been completely enraptured in the exciting story he had conjured up before my eyes, had totally forgotten what he had disclosed to me in the beginning of his narration, namely this: 'though I'm still in hospital.' Now I recalled this to mind and asked him about it.

"Yes," he said, "we'll come to that in due time."

"Were they dishonest?" I queried. "Did they attack you, Dhawana?"

Dhawana suddenly burst out laughing. "You're a dummy!" he gasped. "Quite the contrary, oh quite…"

And he first had to get rid of his mirth before he could continue.

"Now listen," he said at last. "I won't make my story too long. To begin with, they all paid attention to the first objections I had put before them. Rather quickly I achieved more understanding of their way of living and some of the distinctions in their surroundings which formed their habitat. However, I was secretly dreading the moment when the 'water' subject had to be put to the fore. And so, one day, I decided to pluck up courage and tackle the problem myself. I stole surreptitiously to the beach and, after some hesitation, dipped my great big foot into the rolling water. Brr... how wet it was, and especially this never stopping movement of the waves made me rather nervous. But I had to keep up the good work, so after another try, I even endeavoured to put my other foot in as well. But that was defying fate a little too far. A big wave, obviously having been on the look-out, played me a nasty trick, caught me in the knees and swept me off my feet. There I went over, got a ducking, and came up again, rather bewildered. What was that? Giggles, suppressed laughter came out of the sea. 'Oh my God, the sea-nymphs, they had watched my clumsy antics, how mortifying,' I thought. Soon, however, they emerged from the water and apologized for their unseemly behaviour.

"Come Dhawana," they said. "Let's try it together. We'll teach you. Come on, come on..."

Now, you'll find it hard to swallow that we nature-spirits, composed of sheer etherical substances, should have to learn how to behave in water. But as it is, particularly when being afraid of water, we must conquer certain natural laws in order to comply with this problem. Their approach to this was kind and comprehensive. First, they took me out on a beautiful raft, made of seaweed, staying as close to the shore as possible, although they themselves prefer to be out farther at sea. They talked to me constantly in the most soothing manner, and little by little I found myself becoming more at ease. Until suddenly, I don't know how, I tumbled head over heels from the raft, thank goodness into not too deep waters. Laughter and giggles again, they couldn't help it, the little r ogues.

"Dhawana, oh Dhawana," they blurted out at last. "Why do you happen to be so big?"

Now it was out.

They had said it.

Dumbfounded I dragged myself to the beach and sat myself down on the sand, burying my head in my shovel-like hands. This is the end, I thought, feeling particularly sorry for myself.

The sea-beings let me alone for a while, I saw them debating among each other what to do. Then they came to me, one by one, encircling me not only by their presence, but also by their love.

"Listen Dhawana," one of them said. "If you would be prepared to undergo a certain treatment, we could convert you into more suitable proportions. That would mean, though, the end of your former and present appearance. It would also mean staying for some time at our local hospital, for you have to go through a rather slow and intensive process. Do think it over, and tell us when you are ready, will you?"

'A hospital,' I thought. 'They must be mad.'

But then, a chance to get rid of this great, bulky body, those awkward flipping hands and feet… A sudden joy took possession of me.

"I'll do it," I exclaimed without any further reflection. "No matter what, I'll do it!!"

And that's where I have been, in hospital. And that's why you couldn't find me after your return to this country. I'll tell you about it later, for the present it is enough, don't you think? Goodbye. And as always, I remain sincerely yours Dhawana."

14

THE SURPRISE VISIT

Twenty-seven degrees, early in the morning. The sea so blue, the air engulfing me like a beautiful, warm blanket, the birds twittering around whilst I sit here, peacefully on my long-chair. Bor has gone off to the village to do some household shopping, and I am waiting for Dhawana, because he sent me 'word' to stay home as he wanted to contact me. Well, so I'm waiting, Dhawana. Where are you? I just looked up. No, I couldn't discover him on Mount Dhawana, nor anywhere else in the vicinity. Pity, I would have liked so much to see him. Curiosity, of course, and I should have mastered that by now, surely.

Mount Dhawana, seen from our house

Hi, what's that?

Good grief, there's someone sitting here next to me in the garden chair. It reminds me of Dhawana, yet he is different. It's confusing, because he's chortling with laughter.

"Hello," I say. "Who are you?"

Now he's almost doubling up with mirth, and it is so contagious that I start grinning too.

"Hello," he says, still with a broad smile on his face, and now I recognize his 'Being', if you know what I mean! It is Dhawana!

"It's you, you rogue!" I laugh. "Is this a way to approach me? You gave me quite a turn."

"Oh, I'm sorry, Roma. But I couldn't resist doing it this way. Your face, it was almost too much, you know. What do you say?"

"Dhawana, what a metamorphosis! You're still beautiful! Do you mind if I describe you here and now, in my book? I like doing that whilst you are still sitting there, so close by as you've never done before."

Dhawana shakes his head. "No," he says. "You're too human, I'm afraid. And my vibrations are still in a delicate state. You will be able to describe me alright after I'm gone. So, goodbye for now. I'll tell you everything later. Have fun, see ye!" And fttt, off he goes like a feather in the wind, suddenly dissolving himself into nothingness after he left the garden, at a distance of about twenty metres.

I am dumbfounded. All I can do is sit here and recollect this most surprising happening. Dhawana, how could it be him? But then, as I said before, I definitely recognized his Being. I cannot find better words to describe it. How he enjoyed it, leading me on as he did. But there was also a touch of pride in him, or maybe this isn't the right expression. I should rather say he emanated contentment, happiness, glad to show himself off in his newly acquired countenance.

Now I must find the right words to depict as clearly as possible what I saw. Obviously, after what he had told us previously, you must have guessed him to be not so huge as before. And that's quite right. I would estimate him even somewhat smaller than an average human being. Five foot two, or maybe three; I'm horribly inaccurate at guessing somebody's length. His facial expression hadn't altered much, especially as he was laughing all the time. There were those old familiar features. His teeth as white as ever, though not that big anymore. Over his body, or to be precise, grown-on to it — for that's how nature-spirits' clothing actually is — he wore a long sort of singlet of a light marine-blue colour, bordered off with bright yellow. Around his neck he had a silver chain with an anchor, his connection with the sea, I presume. Then a meticulously white pair of shorts and bare feet, smaller, much smaller than in his former days.

How happy he seemed. Dhawana: Be Happy. He was. It radiated from him in every atom of his being. And although I expected him to tell me today of what had happened to him during the time we were in Europe, this surprise visit was certainly the most exciting thing he could have thought of, and I'm glad he did.

15

THE REBIRTH

A modern nature-spirit, well, I never!

It's only now that I'm coming to the realisation that, as a whole, nature-spirits never seem to have changed in their appearances. Even Parma and his helpers still live and work as they have done for ages.

Hello, there's a thought entering my mind: didn't they say during our last encounter that new reinforcements were on their way to them? Who knows? But this is only a personal thought.

Dhawana, fancy! As far as I know, he is the first one to have undergone a renewal, after eight hundred years of his existence here on earth. Maybe he's one of the eldest, and therefore the first to be up for a change. But I'm guessing again, and I shouldn't.

"All right," I hear Dhawana suddenly saying. "On with the work. I still have to tell you my story, or don't you want to hear it?"

"Of course I want to, Dhawana."

"Well, here goes then. First of all, there was another meeting to be called for, and this was decreed for the following night. It was a beautiful night, the moon almost full, a soft breeze coming from over the sea. And us sitting on top of Mount Dhawana, how thoughtful. No one actually put himself forward as chairman, but nevertheless all went as smooth as one could have wished for. Here, in short lines, was explained to me how the whole procedure would operate, and with my consent, they would start with the first stage at once. When I think back to that, I cannot suppress a smile. It was all so sweet, so well meant, but oh ...

Anyway, they soon formed themselves into a procession: first the dune-spirits, then the sea-nymphs, then the shrub-beings — they were the strongest of them all. But for goodness' sake, what were they doing? The last, the third group came proudly bobbing up with a funny-looking kind of chair. Later on, I discovered this thing was called a sedan-chair, but then I wasn't so learned yet. This chair was constructed of some material they must have invented themselves, artfully adorned with flowers, obviously supplied by the flower-spirits, who were still trying to improve on the effect of this contraption. I was invited to take my place in this work of art, and not wanting to show my feelings, I restrained myself from doubtfully scratching my head. So, I carefully sat myself down, and the shrub-spirits took up the handlebars, trying to lift the thing high enough in order to walk away with it.

First, nothing happened. I was still sitting flat on the board. Then some moaning and groaning took place whilst they tried harder, even assisted by some more friends. This went on for some time until I couldn't stand it any longer. Further along the row, in front, I heard some giggling going on among the sea-spirits, and now I couldn't hold myself anymore, and I burst out laughing.

"You wonderful, silly people," I hiccoughed. "Why all this? Let me walk with you. I'm surely capable of that, am I not? I'm too big for you and yes, too clumsy. Let me admit it once again. Come on, I'll follow you, wherever you go."

They had to give in, though reluctantly, for they glanced again and again at their handiwork, and they could hardly say goodbye to it. But they had to face the facts and so I fell in with their procession, which was being closed off by the flower-spirits. Now, before I go any further, I must explain to you that naturally we don't have heavy bodies, as we are composed of etherical substances. But to them, proportionally speaking, I was still large and therefore too heavy. Do you understand?"

"I think I do."

"Good. Well then, we walked for quite some time, and it must have been a peculiar sight, this long row of nature-spirits. And I can tell you, I felt rather awkward, towering so high above them. One way or another, I had to fit in with them, or I would never feel at ease.

At last, we arrived at a place far beyond the places where people live. Here we entered a cave, that is to say a few of the dune-spirits and the flower-spirits entered. The others stopped outside. In the centre of the cave was a kind of raised platform, made of twigs, for the greater part covered with sand and adorned with flowers. I was invited to take a place on this and to lay myself down. When this was accomplished, the others, except for the sea-spirits, entered and placed themselves in a circle around the platform. As beforehand they had informed me of the procedure, I knew this would last for a long period before they could go on their way again. When all were seated and silence fell over the entire gathering, the sea-spirits outside the cave began to sing softly. So soft, so tenderly and high, that it made one listen more intensively than any full-sized music could have brought about. They sang on and on, and although the sound-force didn't increase, by and by the cave seemed to become filled with it, and as it was especially directed at me, it filled my whole being as well. Slowly, a wonderful drowsiness took possession of me, more and more and more, and I felt myself drifting away into nothingness. It was a most peculiar feeling, not at all unpleasant. But as I was well-informed on this before, I knew what was to follow, although at that particular moment I wasn't conscious of that. You see, we nature-spirits are also, like human beings, in the possession of an eternal spirit. The only difference is our physical constitution, and the way we live, without the many complicated problems you people have to cope with. So, what happened there was that my spirit was lovingly taken out of my body. And when that moment had arrived, the sea-spirits came into act ion.

Tenderly I was taken up by them — now being completely weightless — and carried out to sea. There I lived with them for several weeks, first for a short while unconsciously, then bit by bit awakened, until I could understand it all, their way of living and gradually, with so much love helped by the beautiful sea-beings, overcoming my former fear of the water.

Meanwhile, my friends on the land didn't sit still either. In what they called their 'hospital', they worked hard to achieve that what was needed: a new body, adapted to the new life I had to begin. The composition of the old thing I had lived in for so long, had to be dissolved. That's to say in so far that it ended up in a fluid substance. This took place in a hollow basin in the rocks of the cave, and when this was achieved, and the fluid was purified — which took quite some time — the spirits waited until the moon was full. Then they all sat around the basin, and they concentrated their thoughts upon what was going to happen. For days they concentrated, and then their work became rewarded. Slowly, oh so slowly a new body started to grow in the fluid, until at last it was finished. The then still lifeless shape was taken out of the basin and put on the bed on the platform. Word was sent to the sea-spirits, and in no time, I was made unconscious again, transported to the cave, and ceremonially placed in the waiting body. A rebirth if ever you saw one!

Can you imagine how grateful I was? The time, the exertion, the love they had given to achieve this wonderful thing, I shall never forget it. A few more weeks I had to spend in the hospital, until my spirit and body were safely united, and strong enough to start the new life. Those were the first weeks after your return, when you couldn't find me anywhere. You wouldn't have found the old Dhawana anyway, for he is gone forever. Yes, the start of a new life, dedicated to serving nature in all its aspects, with the allied forces of my dear friends. Could one wish for any better?

And now I say goodbye to you, all of you. Maybe you'll see me now and again, and we'll greet each other and know that we too belong together, for are we not all the same children of the Universe?"

For a long time, I sat motionless, gazing out over the sea. We had gained so much unexpected and valuable information from everything Dhawana had told us. How marvellously they had worked it all out. These nature-spirits, they wanted a leader, and a leader came to them from another place, experienced, but not able to live as they did in the realm of water. However, they achieved not only to adjust everything and find the right solution, they also added to Dhawana by giving him new features made to thrive in the ocean. And last but not least, he was now really one of them, part of them, for wasn't he arisen from the combined efforts of their thoughts? What alliance could be stronger than that? It was all so perfect, just as perfect as nature itself, and we human beings could never improve on it.

I cannot finish this book without thanking Dhawana for everything he has given us. We'll miss him, certainly, but then he is not completely lost to us. As he said so himself, we'll see him now and again, and this should satisfy us all for now, and for the time to come.

Mount Dhawana at sundown

ALSO BY ATEM

Return Trip to Moses

The Book of Hatma

(Above published by Red Feather Publishing)

The Book of Jonathon and The Book of Eron: Two Books on Awakening into Life After Death

The Book of Eternity

The Book of Godfried. 1975, Uitgeverij de Fontein bv, De Bilt, ISBN 90 261 3021 x (in Dutch)

Het boek van de Eeuwigheid. 1996, Uitgeverij Kairos, Soest, ISBN 90 70338 467/cip (in Dutch)

Mijn Hemel, wat nu? 1975, Uitgeverij de Fontein bv, De Bilt, ISBN 90 261 3017 1 (in Dutch)

www.ingramcontent.com/pod-product-compliance
Lightning Source LLC
Chambersburg PA
CBHW062039290426
44109CB00026B/2666